The Power of Music

The Power of Music

*Harness the creative energy of music
to heal the body, soothe the mind,
and feed the soul*

CYNTHIA BLANCHE & ANTONIA BEATTIE

RAINCOAST BOOKS

Vancouver

Contents

Introduction

Music gives a soul to the universe, wings to the mind, light to the imagination, a charm to sadness, gaiety and life to everything. It is the essence of order, and leads to all that is good, just, and beautiful, of which it is the invisible, but nevertheless dazzling, passionate, and eternal form.

PLATO (C.427–347 BC), GREEK PHILOSOPHER

Once there was a sultan named Amurath who was famous for his cruelty. When Amurath conquered Baghdad, he ordered that thirty thousand Persians be put to death, despite the fact that they had laid down their arms. Among those being executed was a musician. When his turn came, he begged that he be allowed to speak to the sultan. He was brought before Amurath, who permitted him to perform before him. The musician took up a psaltery, which resembles a lyre, and accompanied it with his voice. He sang about the capture of Baghdad and the triumph of Amurath. The beauty of the harmony, the sadness and exultancy that the musician drew from instrument and song, overcame the sultan and he was in tears. He felt remorse at his cruelty and ordered that the remaining prisoners be freed immediately.

This legend is only one of thousands throughout the ages that have demonstrated how music has the power to soften the hardest heart. Human beings have created music throughout all cultures and all time. The effect of music on the emotions is so powerful it can rally you to battle or give you courage in the face of difficulties and danger. Music can soften anger and bring forth feelings of love. It can build bridges between heaven and earth and between your conscious mind and your inner self. Music can also make you want to sing and dance and it can lull babies to sleep. The universal presence of music has led researchers to wonder if it is a "biological imperative" rather than a "cultural add-on" —in other words, if music is as essential to us and our existence as our ability to communicate with each other and to love.

Music is the universal language and the birthright of us all. To benefit from the power of music, you need neither education nor intellectual understanding. In fact, the true benefit of music comes once the intellect has been suspended. To try to understand music is to miss the point entirely — its purpose is to heal and strengthen, soften and make fluid, those intangible things, your heart and your spirit.

Music was perhaps the first way humans found to express themselves — its communication is direct: heart to heart, psyche to psyche. It requires no spoken language, so language barriers do not exist. When you allow music to flow into you and around you, you discover on an instinctive level spiritual truth, love, and emotion untarnished by the conscious mind. And music is not only the province of humankind. Birds make music, and the wind makes music, as does the sea.

Before the days of television and radio, it was common practise for families to gather around the piano, mandolin or piano accordion and sing together and no one worried about whether or not they had a "voice". People who could not afford pianos made music with ordinary household implements. The result? Joyful family bonding.

The music recommended in these pages has been chosen for its versatility. Many of the pieces work well for different emotions, and there are larger works, such as sonatas and concertos, whose slow movements are effective for relaxation or bringing forth love and whose fast movements are good for energizing, inspiring courage or giving you strength to undertake difficult enterprises. To get the most out of the music selections for specific purposes, make a compilation of sound recordings.

Music is powerful therapy because it has the power to reach your soul and reconnect you to the universe.

MUSIC IN ALL THINGS
There's music in the sighing of a reed;
There's music in the gushing of a rill;
There's music in all things, if men had ears:
Their earth is but an echo of the spheres.
(LORD BYRON, 1788–1824)

Music and Your Emotions

Music hath charms to soothe the savage breast,
To soften rocks, or bend a knotted oak.
WILLIAM CONGREVE (1670–1729), ENGLISH DRAMATIST

Music has the power to alter moods dramatically. It can free your emotions, then nourish them; it can enliven a low mood, help your mental clarity, and even lend energy to your physical being. As you will see in this chapter, music can actually produce mental, emotional and physical effects.

The Profound Effect of Music

When a person is feeling whole and contented with life, he or she is deemed to be "in harmony". There are times when you may be feeling low or depressed, and then you happen upon a sublime piece of music and find yourself instantly joyful, suddenly understanding why you are alive — something that no amount of talk, either with a friend or therapist, could achieve. Singing along with cheerful popular songs with positive messages, such as "Ain't No Mountain High Enough" or "Dancing in the Street", can lift you out of the doldrums in an instant. Similarly, hearing the wrong music when you are in a fragile state could harm you. A common example is that some music can cause you to feel on edge — sometimes to the point of wanting to scream.

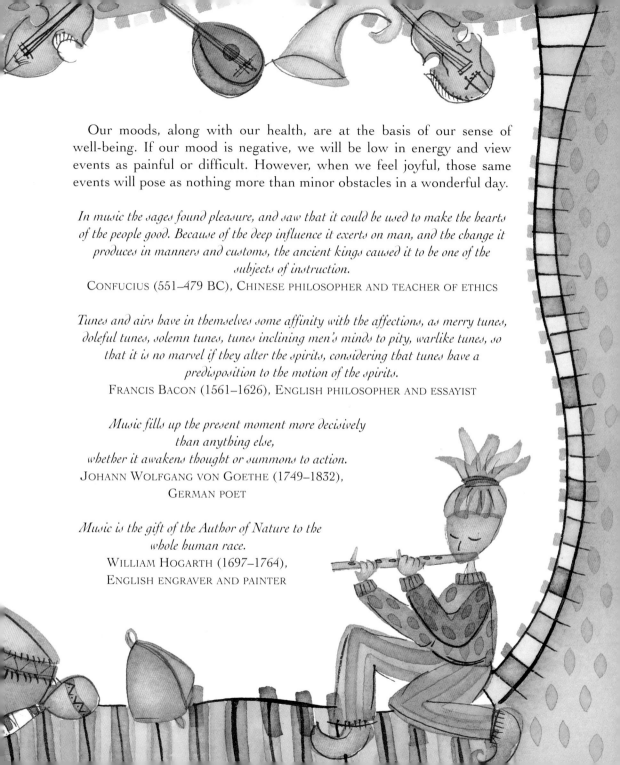

Our moods, along with our health, are at the basis of our sense of well-being. If our mood is negative, we will be low in energy and view events as painful or difficult. However, when we feel joyful, those same events will pose as nothing more than minor obstacles in a wonderful day.

In music the sages found pleasure, and saw that it could be used to make the hearts of the people good. Because of the deep influence it exerts on man, and the change it produces in manners and customs, the ancient kings caused it to be one of the subjects of instruction.
CONFUCIUS (551–479 BC), CHINESE PHILOSOPHER AND TEACHER OF ETHICS

Tunes and airs have in themselves some affinity with the affections, as merry tunes, doleful tunes, solemn tunes, tunes inclining men's minds to pity, warlike tunes, so that it is no marvel if they alter the spirits, considering that tunes have a predisposition to the motion of the spirits.
FRANCIS BACON (1561–1626), ENGLISH PHILOSOPHER AND ESSAYIST

*Music fills up the present moment more decisively
than anything else,
whether it awakens thought or summons to action.*
JOHANN WOLFGANG VON GOETHE (1749–1832),
GERMAN POET

*Music is the gift of the Author of Nature to the
whole human race.*
WILLIAM HOGARTH (1697–1764),
ENGLISH ENGRAVER AND PAINTER

Come Alive with Music

Our brain has the ability to simultaneously, and without effort, meld the complexities of pitch, contour, interval, harmony, melody, timbre, and rhythm (see pages 44–45) into what we know as music. Our brains are "specialized for music".

We experience music while we are in the womb; our mother's heartbeat and digestive processes are as pleasant to us as the singing of whales while we are floating in embryonic fluid. We begin to create music from babyhood when we coo and hum and sing to ourselves. Babies are always blissfully happy when they sing to themselves. Singing and dancing are as old as humankind.

Music has a very powerful influence on how we communicate with each other and on how we evoke moods and emotions. It can help transcend the heaviest emotions in the most healthy and healing way. So, rather than just submitting passively to this influence, try choosing your music to elicit a specific response for a specific purpose. Pages 12–15 are dedicated to helping you make your choice. When you find the right music for yourself, allow yourself to open up to it. You will go a long way towards controlling how your life will be in the moment and in the future.

The man that hath no music in himself,
Nor is not moved with concord of sweet sounds,
Is fit for treasons, stratagems, and spoils.
The motions of his spirit are dull as night,
And his affections dark as Erebus.
Let no such man be trusted.
WILLIAM SHAKESPEARE (1564–1616), FROM
"THE MERCHANT OF VENICE"

Music to Energize

When you need energizing, play music that is stirring and gets your blood pumping. Strong rhythms and a lively pace will get you moving. Brass and percussion are powerful instruments that will transfer their energy and power to you. Read the section "Learning to Listen" on page 50, and allow yourself to become enthused.

Piano
3rd movement Sonata, op. 27 no. 2 "Moonlight" by Beethoven
1st and 3rd movements Sonata op. 13 "Pathetique" by Beethoven
Sonata op. 57 "Appassionata" by Beethoven
Polonaises by Chopin
Scherzos by Chopin
Mephisto Waltz by Liszt
Hungarian Rhapsodies by Liszt

Concertos
Concerto in D Major for Guitar, Strings and Continuo by Vivaldi
Piano concertos by Mozart
Piano concertos nos. 1, 3, 4 and 5 by Beethoven
Piano concerto no. 1 by Tchaikovsky
Piano concertos nos. 2 and 3 by Rachmaninov
Rhapsody on a Theme of Paganini by Rachmaninov

Orchestral
Symphonies by Beethoven
3rd and 4th movements from New World Symphony by Dvořák
Ride of the Valkyries by Wagner
Pomp and Circumstance no. 1 by Edward Elgar
"Sabre Dance" from Gayaneh Ballet by Khachaturian

Strings
Violin Concerto K. 216 by Mozart
Violin Sonata no. 9 in A Major, op. 47 "Kreutzer" by Beethoven

Music to Inspire Joy

The inspiration of joy through music can lead us to feel a strong connection with the Divine, and give us a sense of wonder and delight. Some of the most joyful music uses a massed choir and has an emphasis on stringed instruments, giving us the feeling that we are listening to the music of angels. The beauty of joyful music is that it can help us overcome feelings of depression and anger, and invoke a sense that life has no limitations and anything is possible.

Songs and Arias
"Wir setzen uns mit Tranen nieder" from St. Matthew Passion by J.S. Bach (chorus)
"Ave Maria" by Caccini arranged by Brinus (soprano)
"Laudate Dominum" from Vesperae Solennus de Confessore by Mozart (soprano)
"On Wings of Song" by Mendelssohn

Choral Works
Gloria by Vivaldi
St. Matthew Passion by J.S. Bach
Messiah by Handel

Piano
Piano concertos by Mozart
Piano Quintet in A Major, op. 114 D667 "Trout" by Schubert

Strings
The Four Seasons by Vivaldi
Adagio in G Minor by Albinoni
Canon in D Major by Pachelbel
Violin Sonata no. 9 in A Major, op. 47 "Kreutzer" by Beethoven
Violin Sonata no. 5 in F Major, op. 24 "Spring" by Beethoven
String Quartet in A Minor, op. 29 "Rosamunde" by Schubert
Adagio for Strings by Samuel Barber
Méditation by Massenet

Music to Inspire Love

Love teaches music.
PLATO (427 BC–347 BC)

Music has the power to open the heart. Many of us have been hurt by love and perhaps feel afraid to open up to another relationship. There is so much music that inspires feelings of love — see "Music for Romantic Dinners" on page 76 for instrumental music that is not only conducive to being used as background music if you are engaged in conversation, but also just as conducive to listening to alone. Some arias, songs and operas need to be listened to in silence, either with your partner or alone.

Opera
Madama Butterfly by Puccini
La Boheme by Puccini

Other Arias and Songs
"Ave Maria" by G. Caccini arranged by Brinus
"Solveig's Song" from Peer Gynt by Edvard Grieg
Songs of the Auverne by Canteloube
"Bachianas Brasileiras" no. 5 by Villa-Lobos
"Nessun dorma" from Turandot by Puccini

Passionate Instrumental Works
Slow movement from Clarinet Concerto in A Major by Mozart
"Moonlight", "Pathetique" and "Appassionata" sonatas by Beethoven
Piano concertos nos. 1 and 2 by Chopin
Fantasie Impromptu by Chopin
Piano Concerto in A Minor by Schumann
Piano Concerto no. 1 by Tchaikovsky
Cello Concerto op. 85 by Elgar
Violin Concerto by Max Bruch
Recuerdos de la Alhambra (for guitar) by Tárrega

Music to Inspire Creativity

In most cases the best music for promoting your creativity or listening to while you are doing difficult intellectual work is clear, positive and even in temperament—your mind will take on these characteristics while you create. Mozart, J.S. Bach and Vivaldi are favorite composers among creative people as they work.

Song
"Erbarme dich, mein Gott" from St Matthew Passion by J.S. Bach
"Et misericordia" from Magnificat in E-flat Major by J.S. Bach
"Cum dederit dilectis suis somnum" from Nisi Dominus by Vivaldi
"Der Gerechte kommt um" by Johann Kuhnau
"Ave Maria" by Caccini arranged by Brinus
"Panus Angelicus" by Franck

Choral Works
St. Matthew Passion by J.S. Bach
Magnificat in E-flat Major by J.S. Bach
Nisi Dominus by Vivaldi

Piano
Goldberg Variations by J.S. Bach
The Well-Tempered Clavier Books I and II by J.S. Bach
Rondo in A by Mozart
Piano concertos nos. 20, 21, 23, 24 by Mozart

Strings
The Four Seasons by Vivaldi
Adagio in G Minor by Albinoni
Canon in D Major by Pachelbel
Violin Concerto K. 216 by Mozart
Violin Sonata no. 5 in F Major, op. 24 "The Spring" by Beethoven
Adagio for Strings by Samuel Barber
Méditation by Massenet

Music - A Bridge to Heaven

The soul is in harmony, and has its nearest sympathy to music.
PLATO (C.427–347 BC), GREEK PHILOSOPHER

From time immemorial, music has been used to connect humankind with heaven. It was through music that the deeds of heroes and gods were glorified. Shamans sang their spirits into the world beyond and back again, and chanting opened up the psychic channels within monks and nuns. The ancient belief that music has the power to purify the feelings of people is as universal now as it has always been.

The Music of the Ancients

In 2697 BC, the Chinese emperor Huang-ti sent a scholar, Lin Lun, to the western mountains. His mission was to cut bamboo pipes that could emit sounds matching the call of the phoenix bird. The emperor believed that this would create music that would be pitched for harmony between his reign and the universe. In the Li chi (Record of Rites), one of the Five Classics of ancient China, it is said that: "Music is the harmony of heaven and earth while rites are the measurement of heaven and earth. Through harmony all things are made known, through measure all things are properly classified. Music comes from heaven, rites are shaped by earthly design."

The Greek mathematician and philosopher Pythagoras (c.580–500 BC) applied the word "harmony" to creation. He taught that a fire burned at the center of the universe and was the principle of life. This was surrounded by the earth, the moon, the sun, and the five planets. The distances of the various heavenly bodies from one another were created to correspond to the intervals of the musical scale. The heavenly bodies, with the gods who inhabited them, were believed to sing and dance around the fire, and were encased in spheres, like the interior of bowls, made up of layers of transparent crystalline fabrics.

16

Music in Mythology

In world mythology the origins of music are usually ascribed to a divine figure who lived in the ancient past. The lyre was the favored instrument of the gods, and was the most popular instrument in ancient Babylonia, Egypt and Greece.

The following members of the Greek pantheon are identified with music. **Hermes (Mercury)**, the winged messenger of the gods, invented the lyre. One day he found a turtle carapace. Brushing against the hard outer covering he heard it vibrate. Hermes took the shell, made holes in the opposite edges, and drew cords of linen through them, creating the first stringed lyre. There were nine cords, in honor of the nine Muses. However, Hermes had to give his lyre away to Apollo to atone for stealing Apollo's cows.

Apollo, the god of music, the sun and cattle-raising, entertained the gods on Mount Olympus with his lyre while the Muses sang. Apollo was the son of Zeus and Leto and brother to Diana, goddess of the moon.

The Muses were the daughters of Zeus and Mnemosyne (Memory). They presided over song and prompted the memory.

Orpheus was the son of Apollo and the Muse of epic poetry, Calliope. His father taught him to play the lyre. Orpheus played it to such perfection that even wild beasts were softened by the miraculous strains. The myth of Orpheus and Eurydice is a love story that centuries later inspired many operas, including "L'Orfeo" by Monteverdi in 1607 and "Orfeo ed Euridice" by Gluck, who wrote his first version in 1762 followed by another more dramatic version entitled "Orphée" in 1774.

The spheres (see Glossary), so often alluded to by Shakespeare and other poets, were constantly moving against each other, vibrating, creating exquisite harmonies too subtle for human ears. Both Plato (c.427–347 BC) and Aristotle (348–322 BC) believed that music permanently affected the human soul. They categorized the various musical modes (scale type and melody type) in terms of their effects, specifying which would be beneficial to the establishment of good character. The notion of harmony was intertwined with that of health and well-being and humankind's relationship with the universe and all things.

In ancient Greece, as throughout Chinese history, the belief in the power of music was so strong that the state felt that music had to be controlled. On a mystical level, sound and vibration created the universe, and sound and vibration could in turn be destructive to the heavens and to humans alike. On a societal level, the right sounds inspired good morals and had the power to heal mental and physical disorders, and the wrong music was believed to lead to disorder and disease. The sounds of drums and trumpets rallied troops to war, and the bards celebrated the deeds of gods and heroes at religious ceremonies and the festivities of princes and nobles. But, while the bards were useful in exciting bravery in armies, preceding them into battle, and carrying messages to and from wars and between lovers, they also acted as spies, their messages coded in songs, and they could inflame mobs against the prevailing order.

Perhaps the most important function of the bards was that through them, myths were created and history was handed down, the melody, rhyme and rhythm ensuring lasting memory in the populace. And dream, myth and music are the traditional bridges between the worlds of the seen and the unseen.

Music in Occult Traditions

The word "enchant" comes from the Latin "incantare" meaning "to sing or chant magical words or sounds". The chanting or intoning of specific sounds is at the basis of incantations, and many magical formulas were used in occult practises, ranging from the priestly rites of ancient Egypt to Wiccan rituals of modern Western witches. At its highest level, this practice of chanting is not very different in principle from the toning of Tibetan monks or the chanting of shamans from certain tribal groups.

According to William Grey, one of the most prominent Western magicians of the twentieth century, in the ancient Jewish mystical tradition known as the Kabbala, vowel sounds were originally special sonics used for "God-names" and other sacred purposes. He writes: "Consonants gave words their bodies, but vowels alone put soul into them." According to Grey, through chanting "The Master-Code of the 'Word', A.E.I.O.U.", one could reach what he termed "fully cosmated consciousness"; that is, become wholly connected to the Universe.

The icon of the Kabbala is known as the Tree of Life (see opposite). The Tree represents the ten stages of the universe, both seen and unseen, that was called into being by ten utterances of God, and is believed to be the model for everything that will ever come into existence. These ten stages are known as the sefirot, each sefira representing one of the ten Divine Attributes, which in turn represent different levels of human consciousness. Each sefira is governed by an archangel and has a sacred name. So that the practitioner may resonate with the energy of the relevant sefira and the level of consciousness it represents, he or she chants these sacred names.

See "Toning" in the chapter "The Power of Your Voice" (pages 60–61) for more information on how to practice sounding vowels so that you can achieve altered levels of consciousness.

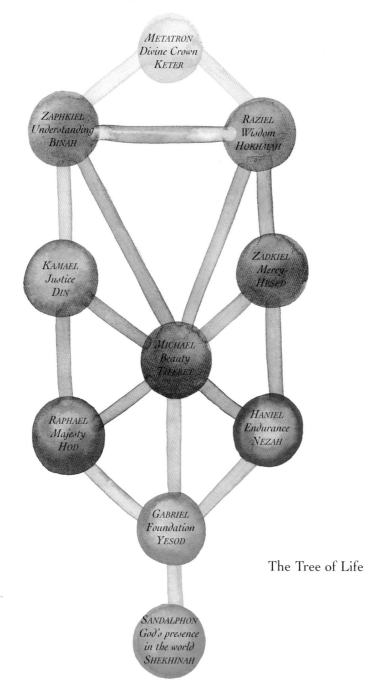

The Tree of Life

Music in Eastern Religion

According to Eastern belief, "Aum" is the sound whose vibrations built the universe; it is at once all the voices, all the sounds of all beings in existence, past, present and future.

Sound is at the center of each person, and the greatness of the human soul is expressed through music and poetry. The ghandarvas and asparas, perhaps equivalent to our angels, are musically inclined—ghandarvas are male musicians and asparas are female dancers. It is believed that the dynamic between male and female energy, melody and rhythm, together created the harmony of the universe. Ghandarvas hear the Divine Song and channel it through to the world while a mystic can experience the ecstasy of paradise through a symbolic marriage to an aspara.

The music from the Indian subcontinent is some of the world's most ancient and distinguished. The religious chant of India, known as the Vedic chant, comes from the south and is based on the ancient scriptures of Hinduism. It is an oral tradition that has been handed down over the centuries, escaping the Arabic and Iranian invasion of the north of the continent in the late twelfth and early thirteenth centuries. It has remained unchanged for at least 3,000 years. The Vedas continue to be chanted by Brahmin priests during their daily devotions as well as for other people's weddings and funerals. Observance of the repetition of syllables, pauses and phonetic changes was strict as it was believed that the smallest mistake could have dreadful cosmic ramifications.

The music of the north, known as Hindustani music, developed as a distinct type from that of the Carnatic music of southern India. While they shared the basic melodic principles of "raga", the influence of the Arabic and Iranian invasions was significant. More emotional and melodic than the music of the south, the music of the north puts a greater emphasis on the involvement of musical instruments. "Raga" is Sanskrit for "color" or "passion" and is based on a series of notes that are presented in ascending and descending forms, like musical scales. The performer is expected to improvise from a melodic and rhythmic framework in order to create a mood or atmosphere. Each raga is deemed suitable only for a given time of the day or night and must not be performed at any other time.

In the East, there is a great interest in the meaning of a single note, on the one that came before it, and on the one that comes after it. There is meaning in the pure and single sound, and in the creative power of that sound. The music of the Tibetan monks best encapsulated this concept. The monks were able to create up to three tones from one long, drawn-out note. There is no melody in Tibetan toning, and when a note moves up or down, the space between the two notes represents mystical significance.

For information on the music of the Tibetan monks, see the section "Toning" on pages 60–61.

Music in Western Religion

Saint Cecilia is regarded as the patron saint of music. She took the vow of chastity in the second or third century when entering the house of her betrothed accompanied by the sound of music. The virgin saint was said to have been able to convert her husband to Christianity, and they abstained from consummating their union. They were both blessed by a visitation from an angel which watched over them until their execution by a Roman governor.

Despite references in the Bible to the virtues of music, it has never had the significance in Western religion that it has had in the East. Music has always been regarded with some suspicion as being somewhat pagan.

The first Christian music came from the predominantly vocal Greek tradition. The earliest written music is known as "plainsong". This refers to the unmeasured rhythm and single line of melody of the Gregorian chants. Used to accompany the text of the Catholic Mass and the canonical hours, these type of chants are named after Pope Gregory, who reigned from 590 to 604 AD. However, the form that we know today developed during the eighth and ninth centuries.

It is interesting to note that the elongated vowel sounds of Gregorian chants create overtones (see "Toning", pages 60–61), in much the same way as has been described in ancient magical practises and in the chanting of the religions of the East. By around the year 900, a second voice at an interval of four or five notes below the melody was added. The simultaneous sounding of two or more melodic lines is known as polyphony, and its development revolutionized music. The Church was not adverse to

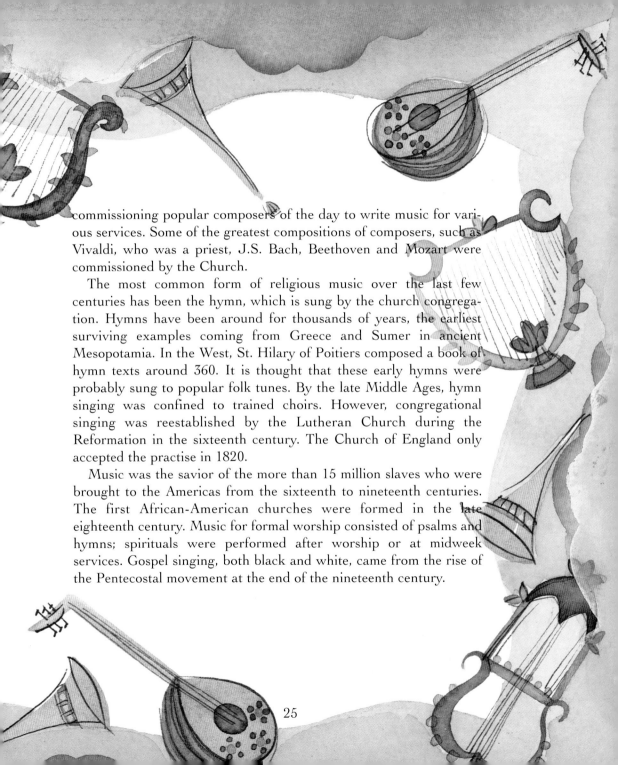

commissioning popular composers of the day to write music for various services. Some of the greatest compositions of composers, such as Vivaldi, who was a priest, J.S. Bach, Beethoven and Mozart were commissioned by the Church.

The most common form of religious music over the last few centuries has been the hymn, which is sung by the church congregation. Hymns have been around for thousands of years, the earliest surviving examples coming from Greece and Sumer in ancient Mesopotamia. In the West, St. Hilary of Poitiers composed a book of hymn texts around 360. It is thought that these early hymns were probably sung to popular folk tunes. By the late Middle Ages, hymn singing was confined to trained choirs. However, congregational singing was reestablished by the Lutheran Church during the Reformation in the sixteenth century. The Church of England only accepted the practise in 1820.

Music was the savior of the more than 15 million slaves who were brought to the Americas from the sixteenth to nineteenth centuries. The first African-American churches were formed in the late eighteenth century. Music for formal worship consisted of psalms and hymns; spirituals were performed after worship or at midweek services. Gospel singing, both black and white, came from the rise of the Pentecostal movement at the end of the nineteenth century.

Tribal Music

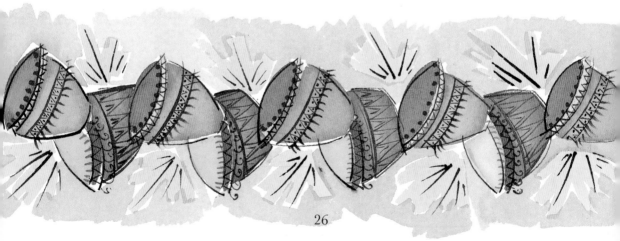

The tribal music of indigenous peoples across the world has a richness and diversity that links a tribal community with the rhythms of their land. The change of the seasons, the effect of the moon on the seas, the migration of animals and birds all have a rhythm that has seeped into the land. Tribal music taps into these rhythms as well as the rhythms within the community.

Music was, and still is, an integral part of village life, where the musicians or the whole tribe participate in important celebrations, such as seasonal rites, harvest dances, initiations, war dances, healing and the hunt. Many songs or dances are considered sacred when dealing with women's and men's mysteries; some are performed by the tribe's shaman and directed to ancestral spirits guarding the tribe. In Africa, music was even used to soothe cattle grazing on tribal land.

Usually the tribe's musical traditions were passed orally. Songs were often ways of telling stories not only for entertainment but also as an educational tool — teaching the myths and legends and reinforcing the rules that bind the community. Unlike the Vedic traditions of India where the chants had to be strictly observed, tribal songs and dances were open to improvisation, allowing the music to be changed and updated frequently. Musical notation was rare, which allowed the songs, in particular, to be tailored to incorporate any new concerns or issues affecting the tribe. In native American songs, repeated syllables were used to invoke the spirits of the ancestors or the animals as well as the deities of the elements of earth, air, fire and water.

Tribal music involves predominantly percussive instruments, such as drums, rattles and bells. The rhythms tended to develop into quite complex structures. (Rhythm means the number of beats in a measure or bar). In European folk music, the beats per measure are often regular patterns of two, three or four beats. In tribal music, the rhythm can be irregular; for instance, it may start with three beats in the first bar followed by a bar of five beats and then followed by a bar of seven beats. African music has also featured polyrhythms — the performance of several rhythms simultaneously.

Rhythm and not melody is the main feature in most tribal music. In African music, some very complex rhythms can be found within a melody that is often very simple music. In native American traditions, music is limited to a form of song which is performed without harmonization and with percussion accompaniment. Again the melodies are not particularly important, sometimes becoming monotones.

In native American singing, the voice is produced from the diaphragm and is expressed as a form of rhythmic breath control following the rhythms set by the percussion accompaniment. In Africa, the melody line is sometimes performed by flutes or stringed instruments, such as zithers, harps, lutes and lyres, but these instruments are played in such a way as to mimic the percussive accompaniment.

The Influence of Music on Children

There is something exceedingly thrilling in the voices
of children singing;
though their music be unskillful, yet it finds its way to the heart
with wonderful alacrity.

HENRY WADSWORTH LONGFELLOW (1807–1882), AMERICAN POET

Harmonious music can soothe and enhance the emotional development and learning capabilities of babies and children. The fact that fetuses can hear sound in the womb was recognized in the 1950s by a French physician, Alfred Tomatis MD, who documented what sounds were most beneficial to the fetuses and answered a number of intriguing questions:

- What music would ease kicking within the mother's womb?
- Would this music have a soothing effect on the child once it was born?
- Could it even help raise a person's IQ?

In the Womb

Alfred Tomatis found that one of the most important sounds to a fetus was that of its mother's voice, and he also discovered that the fetus reacted strongly to the mother's emotions and the music that she sang or listened to.

The ears of a growing baby begin to function when it is 18–24 weeks old in embryo, and they are are the first organ to develop. Once they are functional, the fetus can then hear its mother's heartbeat and a range of low frequency sounds, such as rhythmic breathing of its mother and the gurgling of her stomach. The sounds are soothing and feel nurturing to the fetus. The rhythmic breathing of its mother is only harmful to the development of the child, physically, mentally and spiritually, if the mother is continually distressed or is subjected to loud discordant sounds. Such disharmony can affect the baby's hormonal responses and the neurological impulses of its nervous system.

In reaction, the fetus will have a raised heart rate and will start kicking against the mother's womb in a violent fashion. It has been found that the music of both Mozart and Vivaldi have helped lower a baby's heart rate and have alleviated the force of the baby's kicks.

In some traditional societies, it is thought that the baby can even understand the meaning of its mother's words. Research has shown scientifically that fetuses in the last trimester of pregnancy can hear and understand simple syllables. Consider making up small rhymes of welcome to the embryo growing within you, or learning some simple lullabies or rhymes which you can hum to calm yourself whenever you feel tense or unhappy. These little rhymes will help not only yourself but your unborn child as well.

Classical
Two flutes concertos by J. S. Bach
Lullaby by Brahms
Canon in D Major by Pachelbel

New Age, ambient and folk
"A Gentle Place", Banba by Clannad
"Signals" and "Stars", Apollo: Atmospheres and Soundtracks by Brian Eno
"Innocenti", The Shutov Academy by Brian Eno
"Fairytale", The Celts by Enya
"Afer Ventus", Shepherd Moons by Enya
And God Created Great Whales by David Amos

Babies and Young Children

The importance of sound communication between a mother and her new born child has been emphasized by the work of Alfred Tomatis MD. After noting how newborn children always followed the sound of their mother's voice and tended to relax only when they could hear it, Tomatis experimented with the idea that many emotional childhood disturbances are the result of a breakdown of sound communication between the child and its mother.

Babies who were born prematurely were treated to filtered sounds of their mothers' voice while they were on life-support systems, as well as Mozart's music and Gregorian chants. Hospital staff observed that these newly born babies were able to leave the hospital earlier than usual. Similarly, babies who had been through life-threatening surgery were

Songs
"Cantique de Noël" by Adolphe Adam

Strings
Serenade from Quartet in F Major, Op. 3 No. 5 by Haydn
Violin Sonata no. 5 in F Major, op. 24 "Spring" by Beethoven
Violin Concerto K216 by Mozart

Piano
Two- and Three-Part Inventions by J.S. Bach
Für Elise by Beethoven
Minuet in G by Beethoven
Variations [on "Twinkle Twinkle Little Star"] in C Major by Mozart
Scenes from Childhood by Schumann
Woodland Scenes by Schumann
Carnival by Schumann
Children's Corner Suite by Debussy
Girl with the Flaxen Hair by Debussy
Pavane for a Dead Princess by Ravel

found to recover more quickly, as the sounds they heard enabled them to relax and sleep, and this substantially aided their recovery time.

Young children who exhibited emotional disturbances, including autism, were successfully treated by a technique developed by Tomatis called sonic birth. By having the auditory environment within the womb recreated, children were given a second chance to experience a sense of their birth without any of the traumas. They would hear filtered sounds of their mother's voice or, if the mother was not available, Tomatis also used Mozart's music, finding his violin concertos particularly effective. Tomatis believed that the sounds strengthened the child's nervous system, allowing him or her to feel more comfortable about communicating with others because the nervous system was better able to use and decipher the rhythms of language.

Singing lullabies to small children lowers the incidence of screaming and tantrums and undesired weight loss.

Orchestral

Horn Concerto no. 4 by Mozart
Magic Flute by Mozart
Carnival of the Animals by Saint-Saëns
Peer Gynt by Grieg
Peter and the Wolf by Prokofiev
The Nutcracker Ballet by Tchaikovsky
Swan Lake by Tchaikovsky

New Age, ambient, pop

"Across the Universe", Let It Be by The Beatles
"Here Comes the Sun", Abbey Road by The Beatles
"Sweet Lullaby (Ambient Mix)", Deep Forest by Deep Forest
"An Ending (Ascent)", Apollo: Atmospheres and Soundtracks by Brian Eno
"Beautiful Boy", Double Fantasy by John Lennon and Yoko Ono

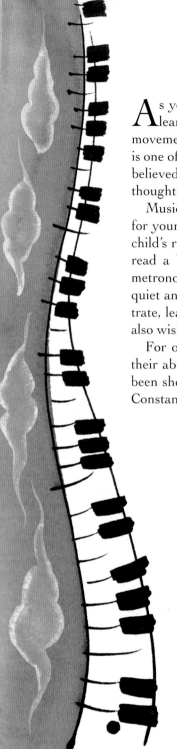

What Music Can Do for Your Child

As your child grows, you may consider whether he or she should learn how to play an instrument. In some religious and mystical movements, such as Sufism, there is the belief that learning harmony is one of the most powerful ways of training the mind. In fact, it is now believed that music can help children learn how to structure their thoughts.

Musical training is believed to have enormous non-musical benefits for your child. One of the benefits includes the improvement to your child's reading abilities. An exercise to do with children is to let them read a book aloud to a metronome set at 60 beats per minute. A metronome is like a clock that ticks out the tempo (see page 45). The quiet and consistent tick of the metronome will help children concentrate, leading to an improvement in their reading over time. You may also wish to play a quiet, fairly slow piece of music in the background.

For older children, playing an instrument has a marked effect on their ability to learn and to express themselves creatively. It has also been shown to have very positive effects on motivation and behavior. Constant exposure to musical stimulation is understood to raise the

level of intelligence in children participating in musical programs at school. However, it is important to balance the stimulation with periods of quiet. Overstimulation may cause the child to exhibit restless behavior.

Apart from improving reading skills, music training also has the following positive non-musical benefits:

- improved academic achievement, including language and mathematics;
- clearer thinking, both linear and abstract;
- stronger ability to create in other media;
- improved self-esteem;
- stronger social and group skills;
- improved attitude towards school; and
- improved ability to remain calm when provoked.

Children suffering from psychological and learning disabilities have found that music can help them release emotions that they have not been able, or allowed, to verbalize. This is particularly the case for children six to eight years.

Why You Should Not Force Your Child to Learn Music

It is important to never force your child to learn music, as any disharmony caused by conflicting wills will most certainly counterbalance the effects of music training. If your child is not showing particular interest, take some time to let the child express what is troubling them about the instrument or perhaps the teacher or the method of teaching. It is imperative that your child feels a sense of excitement and pleasure at being able to make harmonious sounds. Sometimes, when a child is not engaged, the method of teaching may not be suitable for that child. Assess whether your child really needs to do exams in music or whether he or she would be happier learning about music in a much more relaxed way — listening and learning about the dynamics of sound without external pressure.

Studying for Exams – How to Temporarily Increase Your IQ

Listening to music can help strengthen your memory and aid you while you are studying, particularly if you need to memorize spelling, poetry, or the vocabulary and grammar of a foreign language. Research has shown that using light, even-tempered music, such as the music by Bach or Mozart, as background music can also help you concentrate for longer periods.

If you are studying for a number of exams, you can help lower your stress levels by listening to Gregorian chants, where rhythms for deep breathing will help you remember to breathe deeper into your diaphragm. This will relieve the stress because often anxiety and panic are strongly related to shallow breathing or hyperventilation. To keep a clear head while studying, try listening to some Mozart, Vivaldi or Haydn.

Particularly fascinating is the research on how to temporarily increase your IQ when undertaking exams. IQ is short for "intelligence quotient", which is a ratio between how old the person is and his or her mental age. Your mental age is determined by a series of exercises testing different aspects of intelligence, such as spatial, creative and problem-solving skills.

When is the Best Time to Study?

Just before an important exam, do all your short-term memory learning in the mornings. Long-term memory learning should be done in the evening.

In the early 1990s, a University of California Irvine research team examined the effect of the music of Mozart, particularly his Sonata for Two Pianos in D Major K 448. There was a strong improvement in the subjects' test scores for, particularly, the spatial IQ test. The improved effect on the college students who were tested lasted up to fifteen minutes while the effect on the preschoolers who were tested lasted for the full day. It was suggested that Mozart's music had the effect of activating the mind and that the complexity of his music facilitated "certain complex neuronal patterns involved in high brain activities like math and chess".

Piano
Goldberg Variations by J.S. Bach
Well-Tempered Clavier by J.S. Bach
Any piano sonata by Mozart
Sonata for 4 hands K448 by Mozart

Strings
The Four Seasons by Vivaldi
Violin sonatas by J.S. Bach
Sonatas for Violincello by J.S. Bach
Brandenburg concertos by J.S. Bach
Serenade from Quartet in F Major, op. 3 no. 5 by Haydn
Violin concertos nos. 3 and 4 by Mozart

New Age, ambient and folk
Discreet Music by Brian Eno
Ambient 4: On Land by Brian Eno

The Power of Music to Heal

There is a charm, a power, that sways the breast;
Bids every passion revel or be still;
Inspires with rage, or all our cares dissolves;
Can soothe distraction, and almost despair:
That power is music
JOHN ARMSTRONG (1709-1779), POET AND PHYSICIAN

Music has been used since ancient times to soothe emotional upsets. In many cultures, it was believed that disharmony in the mind led to disharmony in the body. It was thought that the laws of health were also the laws of sound, absolutely connecting healing with music. The power of music to heal both body and spirit is very potent and is recognized particularly in modern music therapy. Music has also been used successfully in hospitals to help coma and stroke victims regain consciousness or speech.

Ancient Cures Through Music

One of the earliest references to the efficacy of music with healing came in the Bible. In the Old Testament, The First Book of the Kings, Saul, who ruled ancient Israel, suffered from evil spirits. His servants were quick to suggest finding a person who could play the harp so that Saul could become well. This type of cure was suggested as a matter of course, and when the young David entered the Court of Saul, he was successful in expelling the evil spirit from Saul. It is interesting that David's success was not seen as a miracle.

There have been numerous passages found in classical texts that illustrate the power of music to heal and to soothe. One of the most spectacular references to the power of music against illness was written by Homer, the Greek poet who flourished c.850 BC and was famous for a number of epics. He wrote about the Grecian army employing music to check the spread of a plague.

36

Modern Music Therapy

Therapy involving the use of music to positively affect a person's mental, physical, emotional and spiritual health developed in the twentieth century: hospital staff noticed benefits when musicians began entertaining servicemen injured, both physically and emotionally, by the traumas of World War I and II. Music therapy involves the use of a number of different techniques, ranging from passively listening to specific types or pieces of music to drumming actively in a circle. Most importantly, music therapy can be tailored for a large variety of individuals, including those who do not have a musical background.

Music therapy has been found to be particularly useful for children and adults who had emotional, physical or learning disabilities and who were suffering from acute or chronic pain. One of the techniques of music therapy — listening to music — helps people increase their attention spans and improve their memory. The relaxing quality of music enables people to relax and access memories and feelings that they have forgotten or have blocked.

Drumming is another technique that is useful in music therapy, with the rhythmic beat helping the body and mind find a stable and consistent beat which can make them feel grounded and centered. It has also been found to be useful in helping people's social skills, especially if the drumming is done in a circle. Drumming can improve a sense of community by the coordination of the group's heartbeat and breathing rate with the beats of the drum. This technique is also extremely useful for releasing and managing stress (see "Making Music by Yourself" on pages 64–65).

Musical and Healing Characteristics of Some Great Composers

Music is the mediator between the spiritual and the sensual life; although the spirit be not master of that which it creates through music, yet it is blessed in this creation, which, like every creation of art, is mightier than the artist.

LUDWIG VAN BEETHOVEN *(1770–1827)*

Talented composers can provide a bridge between the divine or great healing power and those who play or listen to their music. Music composed in flights of inspiration captures the feeling of there being no limits and opens a window for those with depression and low esteem, reminding them that the world is not such a narrow, painful place. The selection of composers below will give you an idea about the type of music they composed and the effects their music can have on healing.

If you wish to buy recordings featuring these composers' works, also take into account the importance of who is playing the music and, if relevant, the conductor. Consider making the selection process an adventure.

Johann Sebastian Bach All of Bach's work is imbued with his strong spirituality and magnificent compositional skills where melodies and their variations are woven into rich harmonies. Mostly written in the first half of the 1700s, his music can uplift the spirits and often imparts a sense of almost unlimited inventiveness and creativity.

Ludwig van Beethoven Famous for his masterly compositions, this charismatic composer was working in the 1780s to the mid-1820s. Beethoven's works are characterized by a sense of strength, will power and restless creative energy. His music can strengthen resolution and release strong emotions. His creativity was frequently spurred by unrequited love.

Abbess Hildegard von Bingen The Abbess, of a Benedictine order, composed a great number of plainchants (see pages 58–59) during the 1140s to the 1170s. Her words and music are marvelous for centering and balancing the mind and body.

Frédéric Chopin Poignant sadness, beauty and passion pervade Chopin's works, which were chiefly composed during the 1830s and 1840s. His music should be listened to for accessing more complex emotions and alleviating feelings of loneliness.

Claude Debussy Composed during the 1890s to mid-1910s, Debussy's music is characterized by sensitivity and delicacy, color and timbre, subtle rhythmic complexity and a sense of freedom. Listen to his music to feel a sense of breaking new boundaries and to disperse emotional tensions.

George Frederick Handel Handel's work is well known for its beauty of balance and inventiveness. His music can lift flagging spirits and encourage feelings of success in the face of adversity.

Wolfgang Amadeus Mozart The quality, beauty, balance and elegance of Mozart's works, which were composed in the second half of the 1700s, have been found to have beneficial effects on creativity, mood, behavior and spatial IQ. His music has also been known to calm babies (see pages 28–31) and to hasten the healing process after illness or a surgical operation.

Pyotr Tchaikovsky Tchaikovsky himself derived a great deal of healing from music during his early youth. His own music was composed during the late 1860s to the early 1890s. His genius for rhythm and melody made him a popular choice for commissioned ballet music, and his work runs the gamut of strong human emotions. This can help the listener give vent to past sadness or invoke a sense of joyfulness.

Antonio Vivaldi Composed in the first half of the 1700s, Vivaldi's work is characterized by his ability to hear the sounds of nature and life around him as musical phrases. His music is excellent for linking with the joy and the potential learning experiences that the world has to offer.

Chart of Classical Composers

Birth Dates	Composer	General Characteristics of the Music
1098–1179	Abbess Hildegard von Bingen	Ecstatic, uplifting plain-chant
1525–1594	Giovanni Pierluigi da Palestrina	Spiritually uplifting
1653–1706	Johann Pachelbel	Inventive, melodic, uplifting
1671–1751	Tomaso Giovanni Albinoni	Rich, melodic
1678–1741	Antonio Vivaldi	Bright, happy, focused
1685–1750	Johann Sebastian Bach	Spiritually uplifting, balanced
1685–1759	George Frederick Handel	Majestic, formal, joyfully celestial
1714–1788	Carl Philip Emmanuel Bach	Elegant, joyful, light
1732–1809	(Franz) Joseph Haydn	Optimistic, fresh, happy
1756–1791	Wolfgang Amadeus Mozart	Elegant, uplifting, angelic
1770–1827	Ludwig van Beethoven	Stirring, strong, courageous
1797–1828	Franz Peter Schubert	Reassuring, calming

BIRTH DATES	COMPOSER	GENERAL CHARACTERISTICS OF THE MUSIC
1809–1847	Felix Mendelssohn	Soothing, healing, refined
1810–1849	Frédéric Chopin	Passionate, dynamic, romantic
1810–1856	Robert Schumann	Melodic, emotional, dreamlike
1811–1886	Franz Liszt	Romantic, dramatic, complex
1813–1883	Richard Wagner	Powerful, inspirational
1822–1890	César Franck	Contemplative, angelic, soulful
1833–1897	Johannes Brahms	Strong, tender, complex
1835–1921	Camille Saint-Saëns	Romantic, humorous
1840–1893	Pyotr Ilyich Tchaikovsky	Dramatic, playful
1842–1912	Jules Massenet	Strong, spiritual, emotional
1862–1918	Claude-Achille Debussy	Sensitive, freeing
1864–1949	Richard Strauss	Intense, emotional, rhythmic
1865–1957	Johan Julius Sibelius	Strong, dramatic, passionate
1872–1958	Ralph Vaughan Williams	Vivid, spiritual, uplifting
1873–1943	Sergey Rachmaninoff	Powerful, melodic, spiritual

The Instrument Families and their Healing Effects

Music of the different instrument families can have healing effects on different aspects of our lives. Our physical bodies can be stirred and made to feel capable of strong movement as we listen to a brass band or we can release stress by listening to a string quartet or heal our souls by listening to harp music. The appropriate instrumental music can energize and enhance our lives.

Strings The strings family comprises many instruments, including the violin and viol families as well as the harp. String music profoundly affects the emotional body by clearing emotional negativity from the mind. Strings playing higher frequencies of sound can evoke a sense of celestial harmony, providing uplifting sensations for the soul.

Woodwind The woodwind family comprises all instruments that require air to be blown through a narrow pipe, and includes flutes and the clarinet and oboe families. These instruments tend to carry the melodic line through a composition and their sound affects the emotional body and helps clear emotional blockages, evoking a sense of clarity.

Keyboard Keyboard sounds, such as the powerful vibration of the organ, can affect the soul, sometimes imparting a sense of celestial wonder and invoking feelings of love. The piano can be played as a complex emotional tool, inviting us to release our emotions into its powerful frame. However, earlier versions of the piano, such as the harpsichord, have a calming effect on the emotions, invoking a sense of stability and balance.

Brass The brass family comprises all wind instruments made of metal and includes the French horn, trombone, trumpet, saxophone, and the tuba. Music featuring these instruments has a strong effect on the physical body. This type of music can be used to energize the body or to help ground the body's energies. For grounding, choose particularly melodic pieces for the brass. Use this music sparingly as you may find that the sound will, before long, begin to irritate you, and your body may start feeling overstimulated.

Percussion The percussion family comprises all instruments that usually need to be hit or shaken to produce a sound, such as all types of drums, cymbals, triangles and rattles. Strong rhythmic percussive music has a powerful effect on the physical body by increasing the heart rate and quickening the metabolism. Music featuring gongs, however, transcends the physical plane and can integrate your body, mind, emotions and soul. As this music is very powerful, use it sparingly. Above all, avoid loud and sustained crashing sounds.

Some Healing Basics of Music

Rhythm The rhythm of music is the timing of music, the number of beats contained in a measure or bar of music and the number of measures or bars of music that make up a phrase. Apart from experimentation by modern Western composers, the rhythm is often constant throughout a piece of music. If there are three beats per bar, the composition will continue having three beats per bar until a change is specified by the composer. This kind of music intrinsically imparts a sense of structure and balance. In Gregorian chant, plainsong and some tribal music, the rhythms are free, allowing the chanted words or sounds to form the basis of the music. This kind of music is useful for trance work and other spiritual experiences because unbound by the structure that rhythm imposes, it can evoke a soaring sense of freedom suitable for connecting with the divine.

Melody It is believed that until about 900AD only one line of music was ever played or sung. This line of music which carries the tune is called the melody. Much tribal music and plainsong and many European folk songs are melodic music. Simple, single melodic lines, also known as monophonic music, have the effect of concentrating the mind and have been noted for their ability to calm the emotional body. From 900AD polyphonic music began to be used where two or more lines of melodies were sung or played.

Harmony From about 900AD, harmony was incorporated in music —the one line of melody was enlivened with other subsidiary lines of melody at different pitches (see page 45) and notes related by a common chord to the notes in the melody. A chord is a group of two or more notes that are heard simultaneously. The composition of harmony in music involved the under-standing of the mathematical relationships between musical intervals. Over the centuries, composers adhered to or broke these "rules" of harmony to create a unified arrangement of notes. The mathematical quality of achiev-ing a combination of melodies and harmony is believed to be stimulating to the intellect.

Tempo The tempo of a piece of music refers to the speed at which the music is to be played. Pieces of music suggested for quiet contemplation are often of a slow or moderate speed, sometimes referred to in such musical scores as "andante" or "tempo ordinario". An uplifting tempo is one that is usually suggested for inspiring joy, happiness or creativity and is sometimes referred to as "Allegro".

Pitch This word refers to the frequency of a sound, whether it is of high or low quality. Pitch is measured in hertz which is the measurement of the vibration of the sound wave. If the pitch is high, the vibration will be faster than sounds at a lower pitch. Our hearing ranges between 20 and 20,000 hertz, depending on age. Music that vibrates at above 8,000 hertz is believed to be beneficial for healing in the body.

Music must begin in harmony,
continue in harmony,
and end in harmony.
CONFUCIUS (550 BC–478 BC)

Music and the Elements

According to a number of ancient cultures, the elements of fire, earth, air and water, together with spirit or the ether, have been the building blocks of the world. The balance between the elements produces amazing powers, such as the alchemist's dream of making or finding the Philosopher's Stone. The Philosopher's Stone is a mythic substance that has been reputed to have enormous powers, including the power to heal.

Since the Middle Ages, Western culture has ascribed certain personality traits to the four elements.

ELEMENT	POSITIVE PERSONALITY TRAIT	NEGATIVE PERSONALITY TRAIT
Air	Intellectual, social	Irresponsible, unfeeling
Fire	Courageous, active	Angry, intolerant
Water	Sensitive, receptive	Unstable, jealous, possessive
Earth	Practical, patient	Restricted, unimaginative

Check the table above to see which elements are strong in your own personality makeup. To attain a balance in your life, experiment with the music suggested below for each element, and incorporate the sounds into your life.

Air Music List

Choose music from this list if you wish to stimulate the intellect. Music for the element of air tends to be experimental, with great variety and strong rhythms.

Classical

Well-Tempered Clavier Books I and II by J.S. Bach
Goldberg Variations by J.S. Bach
Toccata and Fugue (for pipe organ) by J.S. Bach
Suite in A Minor for Recorder and Strings by Telemann
Concerto for Flute and Harp by Mozart
Enigma Variations by Elgar

New Age, ambient and folk

"Talisman", Moon Safari by Air
"Flying", Magical Mystery Tour by The Beatles
"Circumradiant Dawn", Spleen and Ideal by Dead Can Dance
"Aldebaran", The Celts by Enya
"Cirrus Minor", More by Pink Floyd

Fire Music List

Choose music from this list if you wish to stimulate your will or your self-esteem. Music for the element of fire tends to be explosive and gives a sense of victory.

Classical

Rhapsody on a Theme of Paganini by Rachmaninov
Piano concertos nos 2 and 3 by Rachmaninov
Two Rhapsodies for Violin and Orchestra by Bartok
Symphony no. 2 by Khachaturian
March from Love for Three Oranges by Prokofiev

New Age, ambient and folk

"Cantara", Within the Realm of a Dying Sun by Dead Can Dance
"Frontier", Dead Can Dance by Dead Can Dance
"Set the Controls for the Heart of the Sun", A Saucerful of Secrets by Pink Floyd

Water Music List

Choose music from this list if you wish to get in touch with your feelings. Music for this element tends to be dramatic yet melodic.

Classical

Water Music by Handel
Nocturnes by Chopin
Neapolitan songs
La Mer by Debussy
Rêverie by Debussy
Clair de Lune by Debussy
Pavane for a Dead Princess by Ravel
Daphnis et Chloe by Ravel
Sonatine by Ravel
"Ondine" from Gaspard de la Nuit
by Ravel
L'Arlésienne Suites by Bizet

New Age, ambient, folk and pop

"Moss Garden", "Heroes"
by David Bowie
Atlantic Realm by Clannad
"But If", The Drop by Brian Eno
"1/1", Ambient 1: Music for Airports
by Brian Eno

Earth Music List

Choose music from this list if you wish to attend to the more material aspects of your life. Music for this element is often simple melodically and rich in tone.

Classical

Cello sonatas by J.S. Bach
Violin sonatas by J.S. Bach
Violin concertos by J.S. Bach
Brandenburg concertos by J.S. Bach
Pastoral Symphony by Beethoven
Violin Concerto by Beethoven
Cello Concerto in B Minor by Dvorak
Scenes from Childhood by Schumann
Woodland Scenes by Schumann

New Age, ambient, folk and pop

"The Sensual World", The Sensual
World by Kate Bush
"Newgrange", Magical Ring
by Clannad
"Nierika", Spiritchaser
by Dead Can Dance
"Cursum Perficio", Watermark
by Enya

The Importance of Posture

It is extremely important to sit or stand upright, keeping the back straight and the head erect, when listening to music. Alfred Tomatis M.D. believed that such a vertical position enabled us to become like a receptive antenna which could vibrate to the music being heard. This also allows us to listen fully and connect with the musical experience.

When listening actively to your chosen music, sit in a chair with a comfortable yet straight back. Close your eyes and feel that your feet are relaxed and firmly connected with the floor. Allow your shoulders to drop and feel your shoulder blades move slightly closer to the spine, opening your chest and shoulders. Make sure that your lower back is in contact with the chair back and that your stomach is slightly pulled in to help your lower back stay in contact with the chair.

Now concentrate on the position of your head. Move your head slowly from side to side and then drop your chin to your chest without shifting from your erect position. Then move your head back as far as is comfortable. Finally, allow your head to settle comfortably and imagine a thread moving up through your back and up through the back of your head keeping you upright. Check that your head is not too far forward — a common position when you have been rushing through your day. Move your head back and keep your chin lowered.

From this position, you will find that you can actively listen to the music (see page 50) and allow its energy to permeate your body and psyche. This is also the best position for meditating with music (see page 51).

Learning to Listen

Music should strike fire from the heart of man,
and bring tears from the eyes of woman.
LUDWIG VAN BEETHOVEN (1770-1827)

Learning to truly listen to the music and sounds around us can help us become more present in our world and benefit more deeply from the healing effects of music. Listening should be treated as an active skill — it is not merely hearing. You need to actually pay attention to the nuances of the music and listen to the notes, the pauses and the emotional timbre of the music.

Such active listening to music can transport us and give our minds a sense of space and pleasure. Listening carefully to music can also have beneficial effects on our body. Some pieces of music that we are familiar with can help us remember more about ourselves in cases of stroke, Alzheimer's disease or neural damage.

Listening to higher frequencies, between 2,000–8,000 hertz, may induce attentiveness in the listener — violin music is especially recommended.

Certain music can be chosen to help you expand your sense of hearing. See the music list below for music that will help you relax into the music and feel its uplifting effects. Sounds of violins and flutes, and ambient music, as well as environmental sounds, such as ocean waves, are effective types of music for encouraging you to listen actively.

New Age, ambient, folk and pop

"Warszawa", Low by David Bowie
"Nana/The Dreaming", Weaving My Ancestors' Voices by Sheila Chandra
"The End of Words", Aion by Dead Can Dance
"1/2" and "2/1", Ambient 1: Music for Airports by Brian Eno
"Triennale", The Shutov Academy by Brian Eno
"Left Where It Fell", Spinner by Brian Eno and Jah Wobble
"The Heavenly Music Corporation" (No Pussyfooting), by Robert Fripp and
Brian Eno
"The Rite", The Mirror Pool by Lisa Gerrard

Music and Meditation

Meditation with music involves stilling the mind to such an extent that you are able to listen actively to the music without any interference from distracting thoughts. This is one of the most profound ways of listening to music, for in a meditative state, you are able to listen not only to every sound but the space between the sounds.

Start the meditation by trying the posture exercise on page 49. Focus on your breathing and once you feel a sense of stillness entering your mind and body, use the remote to start the music. Focus on your breath, perhaps using the music to help you transport yourself away from everyday life.

Song
"Cum dederit dilectis suis somnum" from Nisi Dominus by Vivaldi
"Ave Maria" by Caccini arranged by Brinus
"Cantique de Noël" by Adolphe Adam

Piano
June "Barcarole" The Seasons by Tchaikovsky
Etudes-Tableaux op. 39 no. 2 in A Minor by Rachmaninov
Six Gnossiennes by Satie
Three Gymnopedies by Satie

Strings
Méditation by Massenet
Adagio in G Minor for Strings and Organ by Albinoni
Recuerdos de la Alhambra (for guitar) by Tárrega

Orchestral
Slow movement (Largo) from New World Symphony by Dvorák

New Age, ambient and folk
"Sacred Stones", Weaving My Ancestors' Voices by Sheila Chandra
ABoneCroneDrone by Sheila Chandra
"Under Stars", Apollo: Atmospheres and Soundtracks by Brian Eno
Thursday Afternoon by Brian Eno
"Lanzarote", The Shutov Academy by Brian Eno
"Answered Prayers", Gone to Earth by David Sylvian

Healing Music

Music to help people cope with some of the most debilitating emotions, such as depression and grief, is suggested in this chapter. There are also some tips on what type of music has been found useful for stroke and coma victims, as well as those who suffer from physical challenges.

Music to Help Alleviate Suffering

The powerful link between music and memory is now being seriously studied. There has been a long history of aiding the memory with music and its rhythms. Laws were once written in verse so that they could be sung in public places. In traditional societies, the community's history was sung, being orally communicated between the generations.

Research has shown that rhythmic stimulation for just half an hour over a certain period improved the rehabilitation of stroke victims. This form of rhythmic stimulation was achieved by embedding metronome pulses in the patient's favorite music. Listening to music further helped alleviate depression related to the rehabilitation process.

If your body is in need of energizing, you may consider listening to strongly rhythmic music. This type of music is excellent for giving the listener a sense of courage and the willpower to work through or with any disabilities. Strong rhythms are also important for people who are deaf or who suffer from a hearing impairment. The rhythm can be felt through the body, with high frequencies often being felt in the hands and feet while the lower frequencies are often felt in the stomach.

Loneliness, and even homesickness, can be alleviated if a person listens to music that reminds him or her of feeling settled or happy in their homeland.

Listening to music, especially that which comes from a meaningful and happy time in their lives, is also particularly useful for elderly people with Alzheimer's disease or other age-related complaints and for those suffering life-threatening illnesses.

Music to Help Depression

Heavy emotions and past pain can weigh you down all your life. Letting go of such negativity can be difficult. Music surrounds you with safety as it strengthens your mind and soul. Allow yourself to become immersed in the music and let the tears fall. Tears are nature's way of crumbling emotional walls and blocks so that you may live life to the full. The following pieces are uncomplicated expressions of the heart that can help remind you why you are alive.

Song

"Et misericordia" from Magnificat in E-flat Major by J.S. Bach
"Ave Maria" by Caccini, arranged by Brinus
"Ave Maria" by Franck
"Ave Maria" by J.S. Bach and Gounod
Cantique de Noël by Adolphe Adam
"Casta Diva" from Norma by Bellini

Strings

Adagio in G Minor by Albinoni
Canon in D Major by Pachelbel
Violin Concerto K. 216 by Mozart
Violin Sonata no. 9 in A Major, op. 47 "Kreutzer" by Beethoven
Violin Sonata no. 5 in F Major, op. 24 "Spring" by Beethoven
Sonata in A Major for Violin and Orchestra by Franck
Adagio for Strings by Samuel Barber

Music to Diminish Pain

Soothing music has a powerful effect on the levels of pain experienced by the body. Studies have shown that it takes only fifteen minutes of music to almost halve the need for sedatives and anesthetic drugs for an operation. Certain institutions have found that particular types of music, such as some classical and New Age music, can be substituted for the tranquilizers and pain-killers required by cancer patients and others who are suffering from life-threatening illnesses.

Techniques have been developed for using sounds to diminish pain. One involves the therapist playing one note after another and getting responses from the patient on whether the note vibrated somewhere in the body. The aim is to find the note that resonates in the area experiencing pain. Once found, the note could be sung or toned (see pages 60—61) by the therapist, or an improvisation could be played using the note as a base for some soothing harmonies.

Music can also act as a diversion, giving the mind space to free itself from the tensions of the pain and allowing the areas in pain to relax and heal. Even the patient's belief that music will help diminish the pain can trigger the release of endorphins, the body's natural relaxants, into the bloodstream and give him or her a sense of relief from pain.

Suitable music for pain relief includes New Age music and environmental sounds, such the burbling of a brook in spring or the filtered cries of the whales underneath the waves. This music usually needs to have a simple melody using high register sounds, such as those made by a flute or harp.

New Age, ambient and folk
"The Song of the Sybil", Aion by Dead Can Dance
"Cavallino", The Shutov Academy by Brian Eno
"Bread and Wine", The Passion by Peter Gabriel
"The Circulation of Shadows", Duality by Lisa Gerrard and Pieter Bourke

Music to Aid You in Your Grief

Some musical compositions can be very useful for helping a person cope with their grief. When someone is unable to express their grief through words, the strong emotion can sometimes have a disrupting effect on the physical body. Many music therapists have found that playing certain pieces of music can help release the emotions of grief, allowing the sadness to be expressed non-verbally through tears and alleviating any physical symptoms resulting from the suppression of grief. When listening to the music from the list below, consider using the following affirmation:

"I release my grief and feel peace and love in its place."

Song
Miserere mei, Deus by Allegri
"Ave Maria" by Caccini arranged
by Brinus
"Dido's Lament" from Dido and
Aeneas by Purcell
"Laudate Dominum" from Vesperae
solennus de Confessore
by Mozart (soprano)
"On Wings of Song" by Mendelssohn
"Ave Verum Corpus" by Mozart
"Lacrimosa" from Requiem
by Mozart (K 626)
"Ave Maria" by Schubert
"Lux Aeterna" by Elgar
"In paradisum" by Fauré

Strings
The Four Seasons by Vivaldi
Adagio in G Minor by Albinoni
Canon in D Major by Pachelbel

Sonata No. 1 for Viola da Gamba and
Keyboard BWV 1027 by J.S. Bach
String Quartet no. 14 in D Minor D
810 "Death and the Maiden"
by Schubert
Adagio for Strings by Samuel Barber
Méditation by Massenet

Orchestral
Slow movement from Clarinet
Concerto in A Major by Mozart
Slow movement from Symphony no. 7
by Beethoven
Piano concertos nos. 1 and 2 by Chopin
Cello Concerto op. 85 by Elgar
Symphony no. 9 "From the New
World" by Dvořák

New Age, ambient and folk
"Open" and "Passion", The Passion
by Peter Gabriel

The Power of Your Voice

Your voice is a powerful tool in terms of communication and healing. The sound of your voice can influence moods around you and can create channels for the flow of energy within you. Learning to control your breath to make sustained sounds full of resonance can help you heal yourself and others. Singing, chanting or the ability to make sustained sounds of deep quality through a technique called toning can help you banish emotional and some physical blocks.

Singing - How to Sing Even When You Don't Think You Can

Singing is one of the most expressive ways we have of communicating ideas and emotions. The words we sing are uplifting and call to our soul in a manner that cannot be achieved merely by speaking the words. Singing is an important element in music therapy sessions, where the therapist uses songs to evoke expressions of thoughts and feelings that a person usually feels unable to access.

Often people believe that they are unable to sing a song, usually because they experience constriction in the throat as a result of shyness or embarrassment. Like any instrument, the voice must be trained so that you can control and use your vocal qualities. If you would like to learn how to sing words, it is always best to find a good voice trainer by accessing the lists of teachers accredited through your relevant national organization.

If you would just like to allow yourself to sing for the safe release of emotions, first try just making nonsensical noises or singing any syllables that come to your mind. Notice what you do with your breath. Bringing the breath into our bodies is equivalent to bringing energy into our bodies. How you use your breath determines the richness of your voice. By breathing deeply into the diaphragm while singing, you will find that you will also relieve feelings of anxiousness.

The diaphragm is located between your lungs and stomach and you can breathe into it by taking a breath and feeling its energy move into the center of your body. You will see your lower ribs and stomach move with each breath you make. Breathing through your diaphragm helps you relax and releases stress from your body and mind.

Watch that your shoulders do not move up and down when you breathe in and out. This usually means that you are breathing shallowly. This can lead to a number of health problems, such as respiratory illnesses including asthma, and also emotional disturbances, if you allow yourself to take in only the minimal amount of air over a long period of time.

It is important that when you start singing you first start singing gently and softly within a range comfortable for you. Do not try to start singing songs that are difficult in terms of range or volume. Try to avoid screaming or singing loudly. Do not worry about trying to sing correctly — just sing. Enjoy the sound of your voice and experiment with what feels comfortable for you in terms of pitch — do you prefer singing a low, mid or high range of notes or sounds? If you feel tense, loosen your jaw by moving your lower jaw from side to side and relax your tongue into the cavity of the lower jaw.

If you prefer to experiment with the purity of sounds and their ability to balance your psychic body, read about toning on pages 60–61. If you are interesting in raising psychic energy, read about chanting on pages 58–59.

Some Very Good Reasons to Sing

Singing has the following benefits:
- it is easy;
- you do not need to purchase any expensive musical instrument;
- it strengthens your health, both physically and emotionally;
- it aids diction and helps alleviate stuttering;
- it helps link you with your self-esteem and creativity.

Chanting for Your Health and Well-Being

What is chanting? Chanting is the use of a word, phrase or sound repetitively to induce an altered state of consciousness, ranging from the simply relaxed to the invocation of a divine spirit. The repetition of the word or words can create a sound barrier that does not allow everyday thoughts to crowd in the mind. By releasing the mind from everyday concerns, chanting helps us access our subconscious and our intuition.

Chanting induces relaxed, even breathing, while the repetition of a meaningful phrase breaks down any sense of limitation and allows us to overcome many of our difficulties in everyday life.

Chanting is an important part of Hinduism and Buddhism as well as the mystical Islam traditions of the Sufis. The use of the word "Aum" is well known (see "Music in Eastern Religion", pages 22–23). However, there are other interesting chants. Each syllable of the chant "Om Namah Shivaya" is believed to resonate in different areas of our mind and body, opening a pathway to the divine. The word "Alleluia" can also be chanted so as to open communication with the divine.

Chanting has a strong tradition in Christianity. Gregorian chant, or plain-song, took its name from the sixth century Pope Saint Gregory the Great, who popularized this form of liturgical music. The Saint is often shown as receiving the gift of chant from the Holy Spirit in the form of a dove.

One of the characteristics of Gregorian chant is that it is purely melodic. In true Gregorian chant everyone sings the same line of melody — there is no harmony. The melody is often very simple, usually on a monotone, and there is no structured rhythm, such as a regular beat, so that the music is freed to flow with the words dedicated to God. Modern day monasteries and nunneries continue to use chant in their daily worship. These communities meet a number of times during the day and night to pray, chant and meditate. Psalms from the Bible and parts of the Mass are the main topics of Gregorian chant.

A number of the modern day Gregorian chants have been adapted into English. However, many Latin chants have been maintained. Latin has stronger vowel sounds than English when chanted, creating stronger vibrations which can have a much more powerful impact than English chants.

Chanting
Chants of India, Ravi Shankar
Weaving My Ancestors' Voices, Sheila Chandra
Om Namah Shivaya, Robert Gass and On Wings of Song
Alleluia, Robert Gass and On Wings of Song
Feather on the Breath of God: Hymns and Sequences by Hildegard von Bingen
Ave Maria, Gregorian Chants with Sounds of Nature, Benedictine Sisters of Mount St. Scholastica
Plain-Chant de la Cathedrale D'Auxerre, XIIIe siècle, Ensemble Organum, directed by Marcel Pèrés

Toning - What is it and How Does it Work?

Toning is the vocalization of pure sound, which is usually produced by the voice making elongated vowel sounds. As a technique for voice and sound healing, toning requires no musical training and is a much easier method than singing to use because the person usually needs to focus on only one note.

The benefits of toning are manifold. By creating a vibration within the body through your vocal chords you will feel that, depending on the vowels you use, different areas of your body are affected by the vibrations (see "An Exercise for Balancing your Chakras" on pages 62–63). Toning enables you to balance and heal specific areas in your body and to refresh and clear the mind of everyday distractions. It is also known to improve your respiratory and nervous systems and to reduce your heart rate.

How does toning work? By toning a particular sound for between two and twenty minutes, the relevant area of the body or organ that resonates with that sound is triggered into its healing mode. On that basis, toning can be used to relieve many of our common aches and pains.

New Age, chant and toning
Harmonic Meditation and Resonance Workshop by Chris James
Gongs of our Solar System, Don Conreaux
Hearing Solar Winds, David Hykes and The Harmonic Choir
Current Circulation, David Hykes and The Harmonic Choir
Recording by the Gyuto monks of Dharmsala, India

Releasing Pain Through Toning

Make yourself as comfortable as possible, either sitting or lying down, and focus your mind on the area that is causing you pain. Breathe into your diaphragm and, as you exhale, softly make an "oo" sound, as in "look". Imagine the sound vibrating through your body and that the grip of pain in that area is being shaken free by the vibration of the "oo" sound. As you reach the end of your exhalation, take a second before drawing your breath in for another exhalation of "oo" to see what shape the pain is taking. If possible, imagine that the edges of the pain are being smoothed or shaken away. Draw in your breath and continue this cycle of breathing and toning for a few minutes and then rest. If the "oo" sound does not work for you, experiment with different vowel sounds. Try "ee", "ah", "oh" or "om" and find the unique tone that works for you. Sometimes toning can trigger the release of endorphins into your system to help mask the pain and let you heal in peace.

What is overtoning? Overtones are all the secondary sounds that are part of a single note. They are not usually identifiable by the ear except that they impart depth to the quality of the note. Overtoning involves deliberately exaggerating the overtones so that they can be sung at the same time as the note itself. This gives a beautiful ghostly sound that resonates deeply through the body.

Low-pitched overtoning is usually found in Asian countries such as Mongolia, Tuva and Tibet, while high-pitched overtoning is found in some Gregorian chants. Through practice these overtones can be created by changing the shape of the mouth cavity and the larynx.

Passive toning can also be beneficial in the healing process and simply involves listening to recordings of toning and overtoning or being the subject of a "toning bath". A toning bath occurs when two or more people tone a particular sound around you while you relax and allow the sound to be absorbed into your body. The tone or tones wash through you, giving you a strong sense of healing.

An Exercise for Balancing Your Chakras

The chakras are a group of energy centers running through the center of your body. Buddhists believe that there are seven chakras which correspond with the following seven colors of the rainbow and types of energies:

Chakra	Type of energy	Color	Tone (vowel)
Base	Physical survival	Red	uh
Sacrum	Creativity	Orange	ooo
Solar plexus	Reaction to the world	Yellow	oh
Heart	Love and compassion	Green	ah
Throat	Communication	Blue	eye
Third eye	Inner wisdom	Indigo	aye
Crown	Connection with the universe	Purple	eee

If one or more chakras are out of balance because of emotional or physical trauma, you may tone for the particular area affected, using the vowel sounds listed in the table above. For example, if you had an overly critical parent, work with your solar plexus chakra, or if you have experienced a breakup in your relationship, work with your heart chakra.

There are a number of systems for the correlation between vowel sounds and the different chakras. The tones in the table above are based on the Jonathan Goldman system. However, experiment with what sounds seem more appropriate for the various chakras and feel free to make your own list. There are no rights or wrongs.

If you wish to balance all your chakras, sit or lie comfortably in a relaxed position and visualize a stream or line of energy flowing from the earth through to the base of your spine. Inhale and imagine drawing up the energy to the base and, as you exhale, make the appropriate tone and imagine a red glow "lighting up" that point. You may make the same tone softly for as long as you want, until you feel ready to move onto the next chakra. Usually, you may wish to stay on each chakra for two or five minutes.

Do not worry if the duration of toning varies from chakra to chakra — this is only natural and relates to the level of psychic or emotional blockage in each area.

Visualize the line of energy moving up your spine through each chakra and feel each area being "lit" with its appropriate color and tone. Imagine where each chakra is within your body (with reference to the color picture) and allow the vibration of your toning to find its way to that area so that you feel the toning working within you, clearing any fears or unhappy memories. Do this until you reach the top of your head.

Allow the energy to flow from the top of your head back to the ground and then imagine the energy flowing back up your spine in a gentle loop. To finish the exercise, reverse the flow of the energy into the ground and allow the light and the vibrations in the chakras to dim.

crown chakra

third-eye chakra

throat chakra

heart chakra

solar plexus chakra

sacrum chakra

base chakra

The Joy of Making Music

Making Music by Yourself

Making music purely for the joy of hearing sounds that delight you is one of the most healing and powerful forms of self-expression. There are so many ways of linking into the power of music, even if you have never learnt to play a musical instrument.

If you are interested in learning an instrument, try something simple at first, like a recorder or tin whistle. These instruments are made to be blown from one end and have holes along the length of a narrow cylinder that require fingering to pick out a melody. At the most basic level, you can play a single line of melody. There are a number of types of recorder, ranging from the cheap metal ones to larger wooden ones. Also available are recorders that range in pitch, from treble (high pitch) to bass (low pitch).

You may also investigate buying some simple percussion instruments. There are more and more different types of percussion instruments now available on the market because of the interest in Irish and ethnic drumming. The Irish bodhrán, which is like a large tambourine without the bells, is hit with a small stick called a beater which is available in differing weights and shapes. The West African djembe is a wooden drum which comes in a number of styles and sizes and has an appealing range of rich bass resonance (if hit in the middle of the drum) to sharp, staccato sounds (if hit near the side of the drum). The Moroccan Doumbek is a ceramic drum that has goatskin or fishskin heads and a wide range of sounds.

Tips for Picking a Drum

- Most importantly, the drum must sound good to you;
- Check that the drum is well made and that the frame is well joined;
- The skin must not have any crack and must be firmly held in place — if held with string, make sure that the string is not frayed and, if held by tacks, make sure that the skin is not torn around the pin holes.

If you have already learnt an instrument but haven't played in years, — look at what made you stop. Was it the pressure of everyday life or were you disenchanted with the way you had been taught to play? Did you lose a feeling for the beauty of the sounds you were making? Many people who have learnt music under pressure of exams or other expectations abandoned their instruments as soon as the pressure was lifted. Assess whether you would like to try again with your previous instrument — or maybe you would like to try something else musically. Picking up how to play other instruments gets easier as you move from instrument to instrument because you are adding each time to your knowledge of music and playing.

Consider letting music come into your life, even if it is by pretending to conduct your favorite symphony! Experiment purely with the sounds and creating your own melodies. For more complex instruments, such as the piano, where the melody does not have to be a single line of notes, try playing a number of notes at a time and see what combinations of notes appeal to you. If you have played the piano before, try some spontaneous improvisations that will help you regain the joy of the piano. Improvisation is a time-honored tradition of music, known since the twelfth century when the composer would only indicate what chord should be used in a particular passage, leaving the players with the task of creating a suitable harmony out of the chord indicated. Allow yourself to feel the happiness of playing spontaneously, even if you just feel like banging two saucepan lids together.

Joining or Starting a Musical Group or Partnership

Playing music in a group is one of the most bonding experiences possible, particularly if you all have a keen interest in music. If the members of a family play music together, it can help alleviate family tensions. Squabbles and minor conflicts can be easily forgotten in the joy of creating music together. In fact, playing music together can give a family a sense of its collective self, making each member feel an important and essential part of the harmony of the household.

When you are considering starting a group, don't worry if everyone is not at the same level in musical experience. However, it is important that everyone in the group feels comfortable about sharing their knowledge, or has a lively curiosity to learn more. If you are used to playing just by yourself, playing in a group can be an invigorating experience. Take the time to get over any feelings of shyness. One of the best ways of doing this is to concentrate on the sound rather than on yourself. Know what you can do musically, and let people know what you would like to learn to do.

There are many kinds of groups you can join, all requiring varying levels of proficiency in music. If you are interested in high energy and stress release, consider joining a drumming group. You will usually need to have your own drum, but the group can teach you how to use your instrument, in terms of tuning it and taking care of it and the rhythms for playing it. The vibrations of a group of drums played in rhythm is extremely healing for the body and soul and can even improve socialization skills.

If you would like to learn to use your voice, you can consider joining a group that does toning (see pages 60–61), or one of the yoga chanting groups, as well as the more conventional barbershop quartets or acappella groups. Barbershop quartet is a fun way of enjoy harmonization. With the group limited to four members, each person is given a particular range to sing. This form of vocal quartet is not only for male voice groups — female barbershop quartets are also possible. Another form of singing is called acappella. Acappella singing basically means singing unaccompanied by instruments. However, modern acappella groups have experimented with using their voices to imitate the sound of instruments, including the numerous percussive sounds. The range of music that can be sung by acappella groups is extensive and gives the beginner in singing an exciting way to use the voice.

Your Day in Music

Using music to evoke different moods through the day is an age-old tradition. In monasteries and nunneries since the Middle Ages, music has been sung at various points throughout the day and the night as part of the monks' and nuns' devotions to the divine.

The music pieces suggested on this page and on pages 69–73 have been especially chosen for their specific effects. Feel free to add other titles and artists to your list, and maybe set apart a group of sound recordings which you can easily access for a particular time of the day.

Music to Help You Wake Up

The music suggested below is intended to give your morning a boost. Music with beautiful rhythms and harmonies will help give you energy and build up a sense of enthusiasm for the day.

Classical
Shining Light, music from Aquitanian Monasteries (12th century)
Harpsichord concertos no. 2, 3, 5 and 7 by J. S. Bach
Brandenburg concertos by J. S. Bach
Clarinet Concerto K622 by Mozart

New Age, ambient, folk and pop
"Indus", Spiritchaser by Dead Can Dance
"Web (Lascaux Mix)", Nerve Net by Brian Eno
"Johanneslust", Begegnungen by Eno Moebius Roedelius Plank
"Zaar", The Passion by Peter Gabriel
"The Mystic's Dream", The Mask and the Mirror by Loreena McKennitt
Heaven and Earth by Jah Wobble

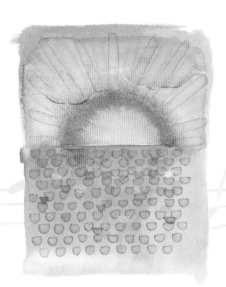

On Your Way to Work

Let the harmonies in this selection keep you awake at the wheel and help you feel connected to a world full of interesting and energizing sounds.

Classical
Dances from Terpsichore by Praetorius
Gloria by Vivaldi
Mandolin concertos by Vivaldi
Brandenburg concertos by J. S. Bach
Guitar quintets by Boccherini

New Age, ambient, folk and pop
"La Femme d'Argent", Moon Safari by Air
"Raining", Ancient Beatbox by Ancient Beatbox
"Mihalis", David Gilmour by David Gilmour

Calming Music for Work

The music pieces in the selection below have been chosen for their ability to help you calmly focus and concentrate on your work, irrespective of impending deadlines. You may add to this list, but remember that you may find that it is not enough to choose the music by your favorite artists. Calming music should not be distracting. Ambient and some other forms of music are particularly useful because the looping (repetition) of simple melodies has a calming effect.

Classical
O Jerusalem by Hildegard von Bingen
Voice of the Blood by Hildegard von Bingen
Mandolin concertos by Vivaldi
Guitar quintets by Boccherini
Harp Concerto by Handel

New Age, ambient folk and pop
"Om Namaha Shivah", Weaving My Ancestors' Voices by Sheila Chandra
"Theme from 'Harry's Game'", Magical Ring by Clannad
"Na Laethe Bhí", Banba by Clannad
"Train to Florida", "Geronimo: an American Legend" soundtrack by Ry Cooder
Music for Films by Brian Eno
"Fainting in Coils", Love vs Gravity, by Peter Miller
"Across the Bridge Where Angels Dwell" and "Scandinavia", Beautiful Vision by Van Morrison
"Visions of You", Rising Above Bedlam by Jah Wobble

Music to Invoke Courage

The music in the list below is designed to help you get into a strong frame of mind for presentations and meetings at work, or for tackling difficult enterprises or fearful situations.

Keyboard
Piano concerto, no. 5 "Emperor" by Beethoven
Sonata op. 57 "Appassionata" by Beethoven
Sonata op. 31 no. 2 "Tempest" by Beethoven
Suite for Organ and Orchestra by Respighi

Orchestral
3rd movement from New World Symphony by Dvořák
Ride of the Valkyries by Wagner
Pomp and Circumstance no. 1 by Edward Elgar
"Sabre Dance" from Gayaneh Ballet by Khachaturian

Soundtracks
Soundtracks by John Williams, such as "Star Wars"

Driving Home and Relaxing After Work

The music in the list below will help you calm down after a tough day and help alleviate conflicts and feelings of stress. The selections will send you to heaven while you have your bath.

Driving Home
Serenade from Quartet in F Major, Op. 3 No. 5 by Haydn
Trio in B Major by Schubert
Nocturnes and Walzes by Chopin

Relaxing after Work
"Cum dederit dilectis suis somnum" from Nisi Dominus by Vivaldi
Adagio in G Minor by Albinoni
Canon in D Major by Pachelbel

New Age, ambient, folk and pop
"New Star in the Sky", Moon Safari by Air
"Journey's End", Macalla by Clannad
Five Leaves Left by Nick Drake
"Astral Weeks", Astral Weeks by Van Morrison
"Spanish Steps", Poetic Champions Compose by Van Morrison

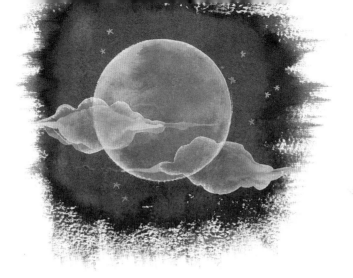

Music to Send You to Sleep

Difficulties falling asleep and problems with insomnia are often the result of a rushed and pressured lifestyle. Music from the selection below all contain longer and slower sounds that will help you slow your breath and start feeling calm and able to rest.

Classical
Andante Molto from Concerto in C Major for mandolin by Vivaldi
Adagio in G Minor by Albinoni
Canon in D Major by Pachelbel
Clair de lune by Debussy
Lullaby by Brahms

New Age and ambient
"Everything Merges with the Night" and "By this River", Another Green World by Brian Eno
Neroli by Brian Eno
"Meditation #1" and "Meditation #2", Ambient 3: Day of Radiance by Laraaji
"Sleepers", The Violet Flame by Peter Miller
"Love Vs Gravity", Love Vs Gravity by Peter Miller

Music for Special Occasions

Choosing Music for a Special Occasion

When choosing music for entertaining or an important occasion you must feel comfortable with the pieces of music and certain that they will not intrude into the proceedings. You need to look for music that helps enhance the mood of the event, rather than merely choosing the music of favorite artists.

However, for many occasions, you should also take into account any special songs or music that have special connotations for your guests or the main participants. If there is a special song, it is best to highlight it and allow people to listen and appreciate the meaning or feeling behind the song.

For most events it is best to choose music that does not have too many highs and lows in terms of volume, pitch and tempo. Music with an even tempo and a fresh light sound, like that of a string quartet or musicians playing harpsichord or other baroque music, usually evokes a joyful feeling. Try to avoid symphonies, operas and other pieces featuring vocal arrangements.

Music pieces for memorial services are also extremely personal selections, particularly if there is a song that the family would care to have featured when observing a moment of silence for their loved one (see some suggestions in the box below). Consultants for such an occasion usually suggest various pieces of church music in the background. For Christian services, often a prayer to the Virgin Mary, known as Ave Maria, is played. A number of versions have been composed over the centuries.

Suggestions of Poignant Songs for a Memorial Service

"Into my Arms", The Boatman's Call by Nick Cave and the Bad Seeds
"The Host of Seraphim", The Serpent's Egg by Dead Can Dance
"The Comforter", Duality by Lisa Gerrard and Pieter Bourke
"Shiver Me Timbers", The Heart of Saturday Night by Tom Waits

---

Entertaining

Beautiful music smoothes social interactions and has even been known to aid digestion. This list features classical as well as New Age and folk music, that is equally interesting to listen to but also does not intrude.

Piano

The Well-Tempered Clavier Books I and II by J. S. Bach
Goldberg Variations by J. S. Bach
Piano concertos nos. 20, 21, 23, 24 by Mozart
Waltzes and Preludes by Chopin
Scenes from Childhood by Schumann
Woodland Scenes by Schumann
Carnival by Schumann
Six Gnossiennes by Satie
Three Gymnopedies by Satie

Strings

The Four Seasons by Vivaldi
Brandenburg Concertos by J. S. Bach
Cello sonatas by J. S. Bach
Violin sonatas by J. S. Bach
Violin concertos by J. S. Bach
Suite in A Minor for Recorder and Strings by Telemann
Violin Sonata no. 9 in A Major, op. 47 "Kreutzer" by Beethoven
Violin Sonata no. 5 in F Major, op. 24 "Spring" by Beethoven
String Quartet in A Minor, op. 29 "Rosamunde" by Schubert
Recuerdos de la Alhambra (for guitar) by Tárrega

New Age and folk

Tears of Stone by The Chieftains/Various Artists
The Visit by Loreena McKennitt
One World One Voice by Various Artists
Common Ground by Various Artists

Romantic Dinners

Consider making a tape of your favorite romantic music, taken either from the music list below or from your own collection of music which may have special connotations for the two of you. Do not be tempted to play a recording that has your romantic piece in among a number of other pieces. If playing a compilation recording, check that the other pieces on the compilation recording are apt for your purpose.

Piano

Slow movements from piano concertos
nos. 20, 21, 23, 24 by Mozart
Nocturnes, Waltzes and Preludes
by Chopin
Arabesque by Schumann
June "Barcarole" from The Seasons
by Tchaikovsky
Slow movements from "Moonlight"
and "Pathetique" sonatas
by Beethoven
18th variation from Rhapsody on a
Theme of Paganini by Rachmaninov
Slow movement from Piano Concerto
no. 2 by Rachmaninov

Strings

The Four Seasons by Vivaldi
Adagio in G Minor by Albinoni
Canon in D Major by Pachelbel
Slow movement from Violin Concerto
K. 216 by Mozart
Adagio for Strings by Samuel Barber
Méditation by Massenet
The Lark Ascending
by Vaughan Williams

Guitar

Concerto de Aranjuez by Rodrigo
Recuerdos de la Alhambra by Tárrega

New Age, ambient, folk and pop

"Martha's Harbour", All About Eve
by All About Eve
"In the Warm Room", Lionheart
by Kate Bush
"The Principles of Lust" and "Mea
Culpa", MCMXC a.D. by Enigma
"Lenore", Love vs Gravity
by Peter Miller
"When Heart is Open", Common One
by Van Morrison
"Heartbeat (Tainai Kaiki II)",
Heartbeat by Ryuichi Sakamoto (with
David Sylvian and Ingrid Chavez)
"Bringing Down the Light", The First
Day by David Sylvian and
Robert Fripp
"I Surrender" and "Darkest
Dreaming", Dead Bees on a Cake
by David Sylvian
"Song of the Siren", It'll End in Tears
by This Mortal Coil

Weddings

There are quite a number of pieces of traditional wedding music that can be played at various stages of the ceremony. The music list below contains some traditional favorites as well as some suggestions that might suit a couple interested in New Age music.

Classical
"Ave Maria" by J. S. Bach–Gounod
Meditation by Massenet
Canon in D Major by Pachelbel
Haffner Serenade by Mozart
"Wedding March" from Lohengrin by Wagner
"Ave Maria" by Schubert
Clair de Lune by Debussy
The Last Spring by Grieg

New Age, ambient and folk
"Saltarello", Aion by Dead Can Dance
"Radhac", Aion by Dead Can Dance
"The Sun in the Stream", The Celts by Enya

Glossary

Acappella – (also known as "a cappella"), an Italian term which now refers to a singing group who are unaccompanied by musical instruments.

Adagio – an Italian term meaning slow in tempo.

Andante – an Italian term for a tempo which flows at a walking pace.

Aria – an Italian term referring to a fairly long accompanied solo vocal piece of music.

Bodhrán – an Irish hand-held drum.

BWV – abbreviation for Bach Werke-Verzeichnis, the symbol used for the numbering of J.S. Bach's works. The catalogue of Bach's works was compiled by Wolfgang Schmieder (1901–1990) in 1950.

Canon – a piece of music where the melody line is imitated by human or instrumental voices.

Chakra – one of the seven major psychic energy centers running through the middle of the body, approximately along the spine. These chakra centers start at the base of the spine and end at the top of the head.

Chant – the use of a word, phrase or sound, such as "Aum", "Amen" or "Alleluia", repetitively.

Chord – a group of notes played simultaneously.

Concerto – an orchestral work with a solo part for a particular instrument.

D – abbreviation for Deutsch, the symbol used for numbering Schubert's work. The system was devised by Otto Erich Deutsch (1993–1967) in 1951.

Djembe – West African wooden drum held by the knees.

Doumbek – Moroccan ceramic drum held by the knees.

Etude – a piece of music that focuses on using a particular musical passage as a study to improve the player's abilities.

Improvisation – (also known as extemporization), the performance of music without having first composed the piece. In some early works, the performers were allowed in some passages to fill in their own melody and harmony lines based only a chord indicated by the composer.

K – abbreviation for Köchel, the symbol used for the numbering of Mozart's work. The system by first devised by Ludwig von Köchel (1800–1877).

Mass – music written to accompany the Christian Mass. There are often five choruses — Kyrie, Gloria, Credo, Sanctus with Benedictus, and Agnus Dei.

Modes – forms of scales popular c. 400AD–1500AD. There were up to twelve different ways that the notes in these scales were ordered. Two of the modes have survived to this day and they are known as major and minor scales.

Movement – a composition that forms part of a suite or symphony.

Nocturne – a composition that implies the romance of the evening.

Op. – short for opus, which is Latin for "work". Composers started numbering their own work from the early seventeenth century.

Overtoning – a particular technique to allow the voice to sing primary as well as secondary sounds of a note at the same time.

Passion – music written to accompany the Passion of Christ (the episodes before his crucifixion) which is performed during Holy Week (the last week of Lent, beginning on Palm Sunday).

Plainsong – (also known as plainchant or chant), vocal church chants.

Polonaise – a Polish dance popularized in Chopin's piano music.

Polyrhythms – two or more rhythms played simultaneously.

Requiem – the music accompanying a Roman Catholic Mass for the deceased.

Rhythm – the timing of the music, as in the number of beats in every bar of music.

Spheres – (also known as Harmony of the Spheres or Celestial Harmony), the belief first put forward by Pythagorus (c.500–580) that the mathematical ratio between the planets and earth corresponded with a particular sound.

Sonata – a musical piece composed for a player or a small group of players. It usually comprises between one and four movements.

Scherzo – a fast-paced playful musical composition.

Serenade – a romantic composition akin to a symphony, only less formal.

Staccato – a note or group of notes played crisply. Each note sounds detached from the other.

Suite – a group of instrumental pieces, derived from dance forms, which are usually composed to accompany ballet or theater productions.

Symphony – a musical composition for an orchestra, usually comprising three or four movements.

Tempo – performance speed of a piece of music.

Timbre – (pronounced tam-ber), a French term referring to the quality of the notes – whether they are clear, vibrant or dull, cool or warm, bright or soulful.

Toning – use of the voice to produce pure sound, often when making vowel sounds.

Waltz – an instrumental composition based on a German dance.

First published in Canada in 2000 by
Raincoast Books
8680 Cambie Street
Vancouver, B.C. V6P 6M9
(604) 323 7100
www.raincoast.com

Commissioned by Deborah Nixon
Text: Cynthia Blanche and Antonia Beattie
Designer: Sue Rawkins
Editor: Avril Janks
Illustrations: Joanna Davies
Production Manager: Kristy Nelson
Project Co-ordinator: Clare Wallis

Canadian Cataloguing in Publication Data
Blanche, Cynthia, 1952-
  The power of music

  ISBN 1-55192-313-0
  1. Music therapy. I. Beattie,Antonia. II. Title
  ML3920.B642000   615.8'5154   C99-911260-0

Set in Cochin on Quark XPress
Printed in Singapore by Tien Wah Press (Pte) Ltd